THE ILLUSTRATED
ENCYCLOPEDIA

VOLUME 6

N-Q

Belitha Press

First published 1995 by
Macmillan Education Australia Pty Ltd

First published in the United Kingdom in 1995 by
Belitha Press Limited
31 Newington Green, London N16 9PU

Cataloguing in print data available from the British Library.

ISBN 1 85561 525 8 (Vol 6)
ISBN 1 85561 529 0 (Set)

Consultant: Frances Warhurst
UK editor: Maria O'Neill
Project editor: Jo Higgins

Typeset by Polar Design
Printed in Hong Kong

Acknowledgements

The author and publishers are grateful to the following for permission to reproduce copyright photographs:

Kevin Aitken/A.N.T. Photo Library, p. 17 (bottom); Art Gallery of N.S.W., p. 29 (bottom left), Frank Hinder, Dog Gymkhana
(Study) 1939, Tempera on lightweight paper mounted on paperboard 68.21x51.1, Purchased 1967; Australian Picture Library,
pp. 24, 25 (left), 51 (top right); Coo-ee Picture Library, pp. 6 (left), 8 (right), 9, 18, 25 (bottom), 27 (bottom), 30, 31 (bottom)
33 (top), 35, 37 (top), 39 (bottom), 41 (top right), 42, 47, 48 (bottom), 49 (bottom), 50 (bottom left), 52 (bottom right), 53
(centre), 54 (bottom), 56, 60 (left), 61 (right), 63, 64 (top); Frithfoto/A.N.T. Photo Library, p. 41 (left); John Higgins p. 19
(bottom left); Patrick Horton/Northside Photographics, p. 13; Gerard Lacz/A.N.T. Photo Library, p. 39 (right); Dale Mann/
Retrospect, p. 50 (top); Northern Territory Tourist Commission, p. 6 (bottom); Northside Photographics, pp. 15 (bottom left),
33, 38 (bottom), 40, 41 (bottom), 46 (circle), 52 (left), 61 (left & right), 62; PIA/Plastic Industry Association, p. 48 (top);
Police Life, p. 51 (bottom right); C. & S. Pollitt/A.N.T. Photo Library, p. 8 (left); The Photo Library, p. 22 (bottom); Queens-
land Art Gallery, p. 29 (top right), Elioth Gruner, Clearing fog, Prospect 1917, oil on composition board 47/60 cm. Purchased
1967; Sporting Pix, pp. 20, 21; Stock Photos, p. 55 (top left); R. Thwaites/A.N.T. Photo Library, p. 32; Wild Nature/A.N.T. Photo
Library, p. 38 (top); Norbert Wu/A.N.T. Photo Library, pp. 17 (top), 19 (bottom right).

While every care has been taken to trace and acknowledge copyright the publishers tender their apologies for any accidental
infringement where copyright has proved untraceable.

Illustrators
Sharyn Madder: 6, 7, 16, 17, 30, 31, 54, 55,
Rhyll Plant: 13, 14, 15, 18, 19, 26, 27, 44, 45, 46, 47, 52, 53
John Fairbridge: 4, 5, 10, 32, 33, 38, 39, 42, 43, 56, 57, 58, 59, 63
Paul Konye: 9, 12, 20, 21, 22, 23, 48, 64
Andrew Plant: 8, 24, 25, 34, 35, 36, 37, 40, 41, 49, 62
Xiangyi Mo: 11
Chantal Stewart: 60, 61

HOW TO USE THIS BOOK

The Illustrated Encyclopedia has over 300 entries. The entries are arranged alphabetically. To find your topic, use the guide letters at the top of each page to check you have the right volume. The first letter of your topic will be highlighted.

TOPIC: NATIONAL PARK

guide letter

N O P Q R S T U V W X Y Z

Use the guide words printed in the top right-hand corner of each page to find your topic. The guide words list the entries on a double-page spread. They are listed alphabetically. Check the guide words to see if you need to go backwards or forwards.

guide word

NATIONAL PARK

You can also use the index in Volume 9 to find your topic.

national park
 Volume 3   20
 Volume 6   **6–7**

If you cannot find your topic in its alphabetical order in the encyclopedia, use the index.

North Pole
 see Arctic
 see Earth
 see latitude and longitude

TOPIC: NORTH POLE

The index lists all the topics in alphabetical order. It tells you where you will find your topic.

More information
on how to use the encyclopedia
and the index can be found
in Volume 9.

NAME

A name is what a person or thing is known by. People usually have two names, a given name and a family name (surname).

ORDER OF NAMES

In many countries, the given name is first and the family name is last.

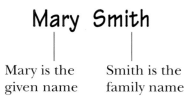

Mary is the given name

Smith is the family name

In China and Japan, the family name is first and the given name is last.

Chang is the family name

En-lai is the given name

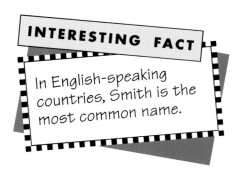

INTERESTING FACT

In English-speaking countries, Smith is the most common name.

SEE ALSO
• Alphabet

NAMES FROM OCCUPATIONS

Long ago, many surnames described a person's occupation.

Smith – family of the blacksmith

Baker – family of the baker

Shepherd – family of the shepherd

Cook – family of the cook

Miller – family of the miller

PLACE NAMES

Some surnames described where a family lived.

Ford –
the family who
lived near a ford

Hill –
the family who lived
on a hill

Wood –
the family who lived
in a wood

Moore –
the family who
lived near a moor

ANIMAL AND PLANT NAMES

Animals and plants have a common name as well as two scientific names. Common names can vary from place to place. This is confusing for people. The scientific names are the same all over the world. Scientists use the scientific names to put all living things in groups. Each group is made up of plants or animals that are similar.

• The first name is called the genus name. This represents the family group name.

• The second name is called the species name. This represents the particular kind of plant or animal.

PEN NAMES

Some people have a made-up name called a pseudonym. Many writers use a made-up name.

Members of the genus or family group *canis*

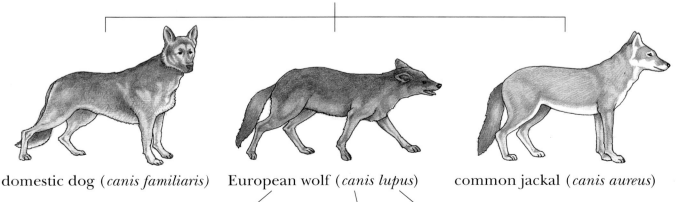

domestic dog (*canis familiaris*)   European wolf (*canis lupus*)   common jackal (*canis aureus*)

common name   genus   species

5

NATIONAL PARK

SEE ALSO
• Conservation
• Endangered Species

A national park is an area set aside to protect animals and plants in the places where they live.

NATIONAL PARKS FOR PEOPLE

Many national parks have picnic grounds, camping areas and walking trails which are used by large numbers of people.

National parks have different purposes.
- They are used for scientific and medical research which helps to protect wildlife.
- People can relax and enjoy the clean air, water and scenery in national parks.
- National parks protect the wildlife and natural environment for future generations.

KAKADU NATIONAL PARK

Kakadu National Park is the largest national park in Australia. Aboriginal people have been living in Kakadu for over 20 000 years. Rock paintings show how they lived. Walkways and platforms allow visitors to view the paintings without damaging them.

ENDANGERED ANIMALS

National parks and reserves have been
set up around the world to save
endangered animals.

elephant

polar bear

seal

walrus

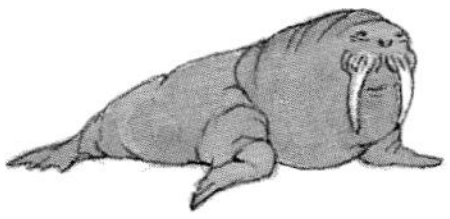

alligator

giant tortoise

buffalo

moose

jaguar

thorny devil

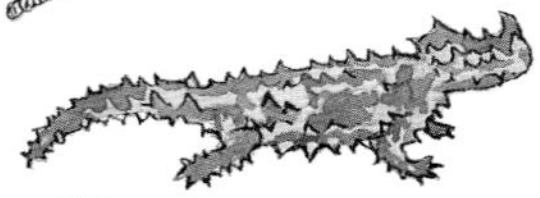

bear

MARINE PARKS AND RESERVES

Marine parks and reserves protect a wide
variety of wildlife – sea creatures, sea birds
and the unusual plants and animals that live
on the seashore.

The Great Barrier
Reef Marine Park
in Australia
protects the Great
Barrier Reef. This
is the largest group
of coral reefs in
the world.

NEST

SEE ALSO • Alligator • Ant • Bee • Bird • Turtle

A nest is a home built by an animal.
Some animals look after their young in a nest.

MAMMALS' NESTS ▼

Some mammals, such as mice and possums, build a simple nest for their young.

INSECTS' NESTS

Bees, wasps and termites live in large groups called colonies. They build large nests with many chambers. Termites build large mud mounds.

BIRDS' NESTS

Birds build nests of different shapes and sizes.

Finches build an oval nest with a side entrance.

Coots build their nests on piles of stones or sticks raised out of the water.

Wagtails build a cup-shaped grass nest covered with spiders' webs.

Hawks build a solid platform of sticks.

NETBALL

SEE ALSO • Basketball

Netball is a team game. It is similar to basketball. Players throw a ball through a net on a ring.

EQUIPMENT

netball

uniforms – each team has its own uniform

netball shoes have soles that prevent slipping

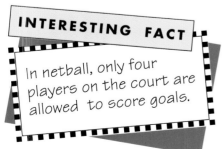

INTERESTING FACT

In netball, only four players on the court are allowed to score goals.

SCORING

Each team has seven members. They try to win points by throwing the ball into the net at the other team's end of the court.

PLAYING AREAS

Each player is only allowed in certain areas of the court. Players wear vests with letters on. The umpire can then tell if a player is in the wrong area. Netball players are not allowed to carry the ball. When holding the ball, the player can turn in any direction, as long as she keeps one foot on the same spot.

NEWSPAPER

SEE ALSO • Book • Library • Pape • Printing

A newspaper is large sheets of paper with news reports printed on them. Newspapers contain local, national and world news.

PARTS OF A NEWSPAPER

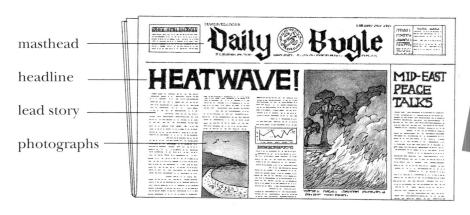

masthead
headline
lead story
photographs

INTERESTING FACT

Hundreds of years ago, town criers walked the streets of towns ringing their bells and telling people the news. In the 1700s, the first newspapers appeared.

HOW A NEWSPAPER IS MADE

1. The editor is in charge of a newspaper and decides which stories to include.

2. Reporters investigate and write news reports.

3. Photographers take photographs that illustrate the news.

4. Compilers set the pages of the newspaper on the computer.

5. Pictures are placed on the pages.

6. Sub-editors check each story.

7. The newspaper is printed.

8. Newspapers are delivered.

NOSE

SEE ALSO
• Human Body • Lungs
• Taste

Your nose is a part of your body.
You use your nose to breathe and smell.

PARTS OF THE NOSE

The nasal cavity is lined with sticky mucus to trap dust and bacteria.

The nose makes the air warm as it passes into the lungs.

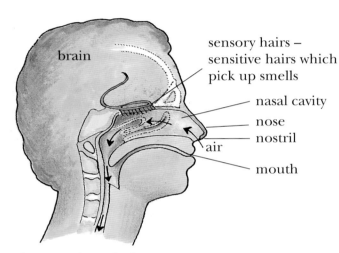

brain

sensory hairs – sensitive hairs which pick up smells

nasal cavity
nose
nostril
air
mouth

air moves into the lungs

HOW WE SMELL

• Smells float in the air. When we breathe in, smells travel up our nostrils.
• In the nose, the smells are picked up by smell sensors.
• Nerve cells in the smell sensors send signals to the brain which tell us what we are smelling.

ANIMAL NOSES ▶
Animals use their noses:
• to find mates
• to track down food
• to smell danger.

TASTE AND SMELL

• When you eat something, your sense of smell helps you taste the flavour.
• When you have a cold, the sensory hairs are covered with mucus. You cannot pick up smells and you lose your sense of taste.

ANIMALS THAT LIVE IN WATER
Frogs, crocodiles and hippopotamuses all breathe air and live in water. They have noses that stick out of the water when they are under the water.

frog

crocodile

hippopotamus

NUMBER

SEE ALSO
• Clock • Fraction
• Measurement

A number is a symbol which tells you how many people or objects there are.

NUMERALS
Numerals are names for numbers. We can use letters or numbers (five or 5).

Today, most people use the Hindu-Arabic System. This is called the decimal system. This system is based on ten numerals called digits.

0 1 2 3 4 5 6 7 8 9

These ten symbols can represent any number.

HISTORY
All great civilizations have had their own way of representing and writing numbers.

	1	2	3	4	5	6	7	8	9	10
Arabic	1	2	3	4	5	6	7	8	9	10
Babylonian	Y	YY	YYY	YYYY	YYYYY	YYYYYY	YYYYYYY	YYYYYYYY	YYYYYYYYY	◄
Greek	A	B	Γ	Δ	E	Z	H	Θ	I	K
Roman	I	II	III	IV	V	VI	VII	VIII	IX	X
Chinese	一	二	三	四	五	六	七	八	九	十
Mayan	•	••	•••	••••	—	∸	∺	⋮	⋰	≡
Indian	१	२	३	४	५	६	७	८	९	

ORDINAL NUMBERS
Ordinal numbers indicate the order in which things happen.

first second third fourth fifth sixth seventh eighth ninth tenth

NUT

| SEE ALSO | • Flower • Food • Fruit • Plant • Tree |

A nut is a kind of fruit. Most nuts have a hard wooden shell which protects the soft seed inside.

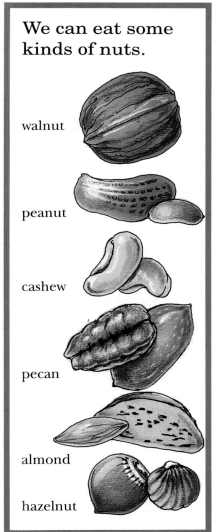

We can eat some kinds of nuts.

walnut

peanut

cashew

pecan

almond

hazelnut

VALUABLE FOOD

Many nuts are rich in protein and fats. We can eat nuts raw or processed in other foods.

cake

packet of nuts

Peanut Butter

just nuts
500g

peanut butter

chocolate

FOOD FOR ANIMALS ▼

Many animals eat nuts. Squirrels store nuts and eat them during the cold winter months.

INTERESTING FACT

The kernel is the seed which is inside the nut.

OCEAN

SEE ALSO • Continent • Fish • Fishing • Tides • Water

An ocean is a large area of water. Oceans cover 70 per cent of the Earth's surface. The oceans of the world contain over 90 per cent of the Earth's water.

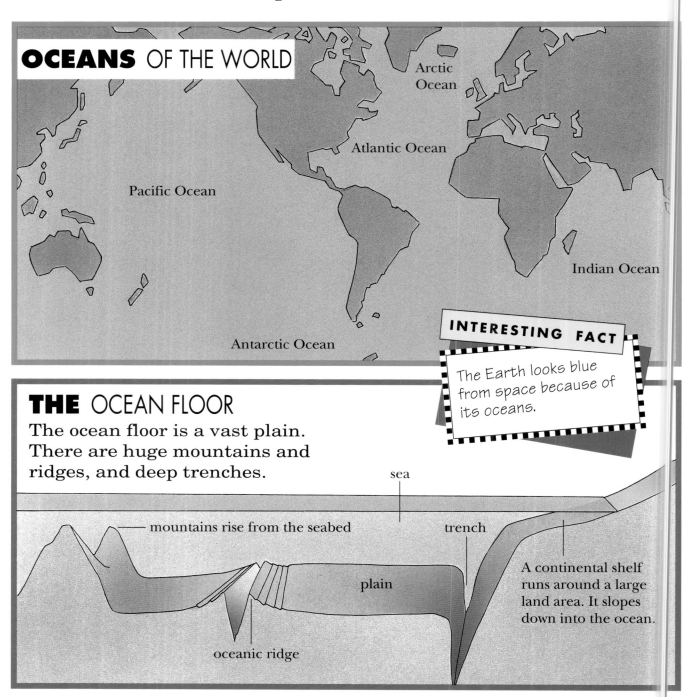

OCEANS OF THE WORLD

Arctic Ocean

Atlantic Ocean

Pacific Ocean

Indian Ocean

Antarctic Ocean

INTERESTING FACT

The Earth looks blue from space because of its oceans.

THE OCEAN FLOOR

The ocean floor is a vast plain. There are huge mountains and ridges, and deep trenches.

sea

mountains rise from the seabed

trench

plain

A continental shelf runs around a large land area. It slopes down into the ocean.

oceanic ridge

MOVEMENT OF THE OCEANS

Oceans are always moving.

- Tides rise and fall every 12 hours.
- Currents are regular paths along which ocean waters move. There are warm and cold currents.
- Currents are caused by wind and warm water moving away from the equator. Cold water from the polar regions flows in to replace it.

OCEAN LIFE

Many different kinds of plants and animals live in the ocean. Many other animals depend on the ocean for survival.

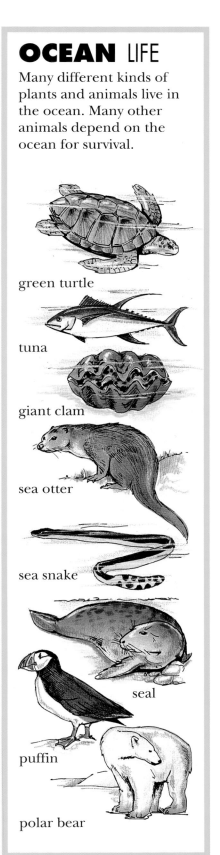

green turtle

tuna

giant clam

sea otter

sea snake

seal

puffin

polar bear

OCEAN RESEARCH

Scientists study the ocean. They use ships as laboratories.

PLANKTON

Plankton are tiny single-celled plants and animals that drift about in the ocean. All sea animals either feed on plankton or on the animals that eat plankton.

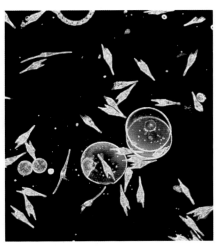

OCTOPUS

SEE ALSO
- Animal • Mollusc
- Invertebrate • Oyster

An octopus is a sea animal. It has a soft body and eight arms called tentacles.

PARTS OF AN OCTOPUS

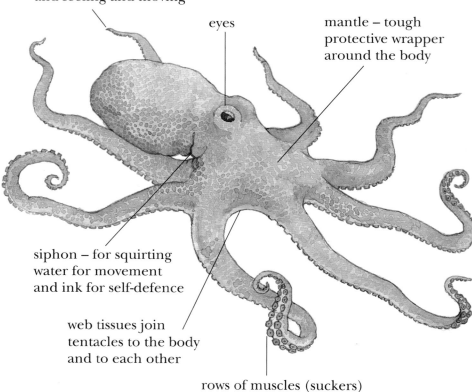

8 tentacles for catching food and feeling and moving

eyes

mantle – tough protective wrapper around the body

siphon – for squirting water for movement and ink for self-defence

web tissues join tentacles to the body and to each other

rows of muscles (suckers)

Width: 4 centimetres to 9 metres across tentacles

INTERESTING FACT

If an octopus loses a tentacle, another grows in its place.

FOOD

Octopuses eat other animals. They are carnivores. Some kinds of octopus inject their prey with poison that paralyses them.

crabs

shellfish

small fish

WHERE OCTOPUSES LIVE

- ● China Sea
- ■ Mediterranean Sea
- ◆ Hawaii
- ★ North America
- ▲ Australia
- ▼ West Indies
- ✳ New Zealand

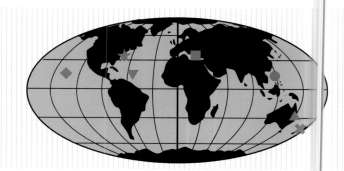

16

OCTOPUSES, SQUID AND CUTTLEFISH

Squid, cuttlefish and octopuses are molluscs. Unlike other molluscs, they do not have a shell outside their bodies.

- Cuttlefish and squid have a shell inside their bodies.
- Octopuses do not have a shell or bones inside their bodies.

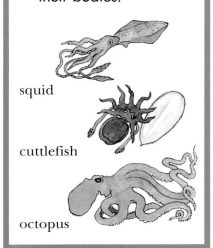

squid

cuttlefish

octopus

HOW AN OCTOPUS LIVES

- Octopuses live in sea caves and rock pools. They come out at night to hunt for food.
- Many octopuses can change colour to blend with their surroundings.
- The female octopus lays about 180 000 transparent eggs. The eggs become attached to rocks and hatch in about two months. The female octopus cares for the eggs during this time. The young octopuses find their own food as soon as they hatch.

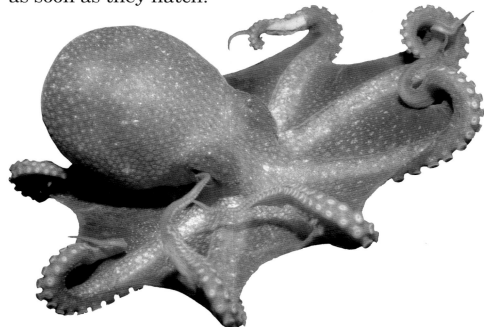

OCTOPUS INK

An octopus can escape from its enemies by squirting a cloud of dark fluid like ink into the water. The dark fluid comes out of the octopus's siphon.

INTERESTING FACT

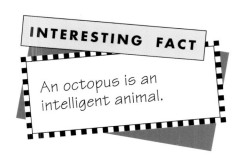

An octopus is an intelligent animal.

HOW AN OCTOPUS MOVES

An octopus crawls over rocks and other objects using its tentacles. It can swim backwards by forcing a jet of water out through its siphon.

SEE ALSO   • Fossil • Fuel • Pollution

OIL

Oil is a greasy liquid. There are many different kinds of oil. Mineral oils are found underground. Vegetable oils are made from plants.

MINERAL OIL

Mineral oil is found underground. An oil rig is set up above an oil well. It supports the drill as it cuts into the rock below.

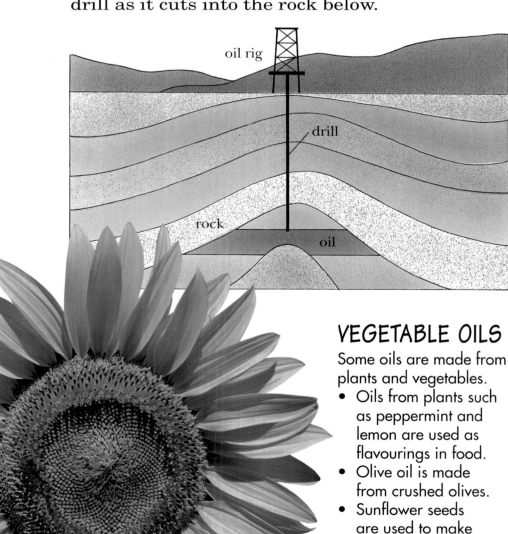

oil rig

drill

rock

oil

VEGETABLE OILS

Some oils are made from plants and vegetables.
- Oils from plants such as peppermint and lemon are used as flavourings in food.
- Olive oil is made from crushed olives.
- Sunflower seeds are used to make sunflower oil.

USES OF OIL

Oil is used for many things.

cooking oil

paint

margarine

perfume and cosmetics

soap

furniture polish

nylon

petrol

fertilizer

plastic

diesel oil

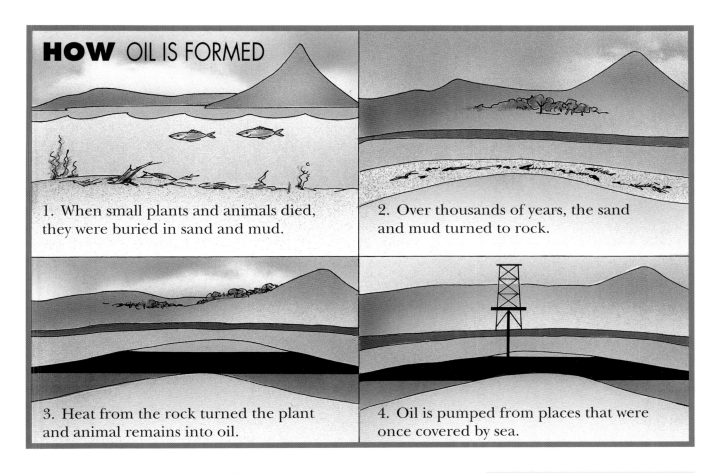

HOW OIL IS FORMED

1. When small plants and animals died, they were buried in sand and mud.

2. Over thousands of years, the sand and mud turned to rock.

3. Heat from the rock turned the plant and animal remains into oil.

4. Oil is pumped from places that were once covered by sea.

PETROLEUM AND OTHER FUELS

Oil is treated at oil refineries to make petrol and other fuels such as diesel. Oil is also used to make chemicals, bitumen and oil for lubrication.

OIL POLLUTION

Oil tankers are large ships that carry oil. Oil that leaks from tankers damages sea life and pollutes the shore.

OLYMPIC GAMES

SEE ALSO • Athletics • Flag • Gymnastics • Water Sports

The Olympic Games are an important and popular sporting contest. They are held every four years. Most countries send their best athletes and teams to take part in more than 20 different sports.

HISTORY

The first Olympic Games were held in ancient Greece more than 2000 years ago. The modern Olympics began in Athens, Greece, in 1896.

◄ THE OLYMPIC SYMBOL

The Olympic symbol is made up of five rings that are joined or interlocked. The rings are coloured blue, yellow, black, green and red.

THE OLYMPIC FLAME

The Olympic flame is a symbol of peace and friendship. It is lit for the opening ceremony. Teams of runners carry the lighted torch from Olympia, in Greece, to the place where the games are to be held. Olympia was the place where the ancient games were held.

OLYMPIC MEDALS

Individuals and teams compete for medals, and for the honour and glory of taking part in the Olympic Games.

gold medal   silver medal   bronze medal
1st place   2nd place   3rd place

◀ **WINTER** OLYMPICS

The Olympic Winter Games are held separately from the Summer Games. Since 1994, the Winter Olympics and Summer Olympics are held two years apart. Competitors take part in events such as skating and ski jumping.

OLYMPIC SPORTS

Many sports such as jumping, running, gymnastics and swimming are included in the Olympic Games.

javelin   hockey   running   canoeing   archery

long jump   swimming   high jump   gymnastics   sailing

ORCHESTRA

SEE ALSO • Ballet • Bell • Dance • Music • Xylophone

An orchestra is a large group of musicians who play musical instruments together. Most orchestras have a conductor to lead them.

The strings are the most important group of instruments in an orchestra. Strings make up two-thirds of the instruments in most orchestras.

THE CONDUCTOR ▶
The conductor uses signs to guide the musicians when playing music.

SOME INSTRUMENTS IN AN ORCHESTRA

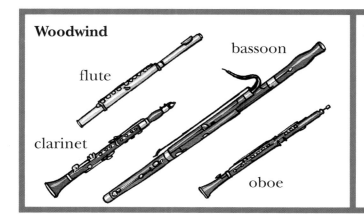

Woodwind

flute
bassoon
clarinet
oboe

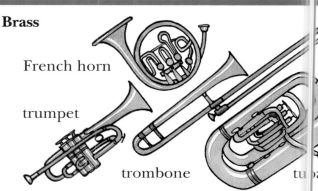

Brass

French horn
trumpet
trombone
tuba

WHERE DIFFERENT PLAYERS SIT

Usually, musicians playing the same kind of musical instrument sit together.

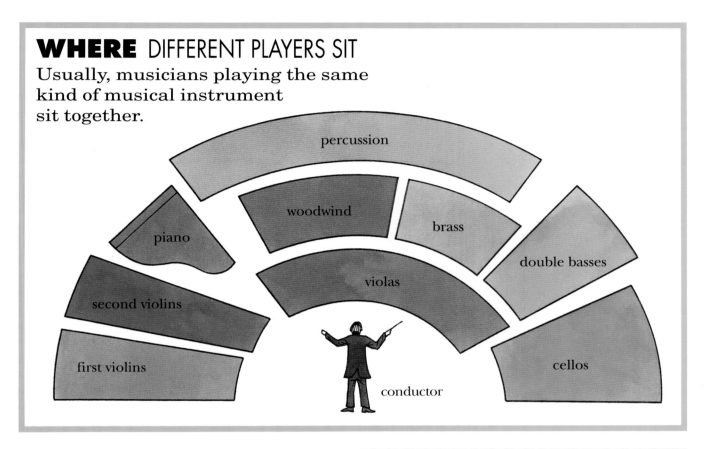

WHAT ORCHESTRAS PLAY

- A symphony is a piece of music just for an orchestra.
- A concerto is a piece of music for an orchestra and a solo instrument.
- Orchestras play music to accompany individual singers and choirs.
- Orchestras play music for operas, ballets and musicals.

KINDS OF ORCHESTRAS

There are many different kinds of orchestras. A dance orchestra plays music for dancing and listening. A chamber orchestra only has stringed instruments. It plays music which is especially written for it.

String

Percussion

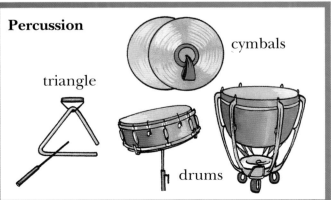

OSTRICH

SEE ALSO • Animal • Bird

An ostrich is the largest bird on Earth.
Ostriches cannot fly, but they can run very fast.

PARTS OF AN OSTRICH

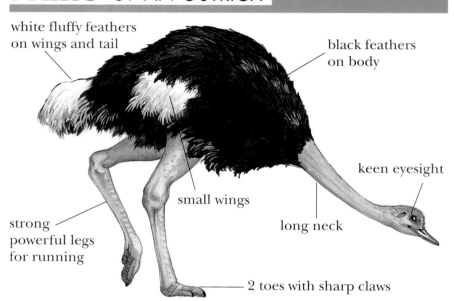

white fluffy feathers on wings and tail

black feathers on body

small wings

keen eyesight

strong powerful legs for running

long neck

2 toes with sharp claws

Average height: 2.5 metres
Average weight: 135 kilograms

FOOD

mostly plants

turtles

lizards

WHERE OSTRICHES LIVE

● **Africa**

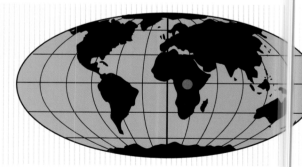

HOW OSTRICHES LIVE

Ostriches roam in herds. They dig shallow nests in sand. The female ostrich lays 10 to 15 large eggs. Several female ostriches lay their eggs in the same nest. The eggs hatch in four to six weeks. The young ostriches can run very fast and feed themselves.

SEE ALSO | • Animal • Bird

OWL

An owl is a hunting bird. Owls hunt at night.
They live in all parts of the world.

PARTS OF A COMMON OWL

ruff of feathers
large forward-looking eyes
thick body
large wings
head can turn right around to look backwards
hooked beak for eating prey
soft feathers
hooked talons for catching prey

Length: 32 to 35 centimetres

FOOD

rats
mice
rabbits
squirrels
frogs
smaller birds

OWL PELLETS

Owl pellets are found under an owl's roosting place. When an owl eats mice or birds and other prey, it swallows bones, feathers and fur. Later, the owl coughs up the undigested remains in pellets.

HOW OWLS LIVE

Owls usually lay three to four white eggs. They make rough nests in holes in trees, on ledges on buildings or in burrows in the ground. Both male and female owls help to care for their eggs and young.

25

OYSTER

SEE ALSO • Animal • Mollusc • Ocean

An oyster is a sea animal. Its soft, grey body is protected inside two hinged shells. The shells are rough and hard on the outside, and smooth and shiny on the inside.

PARTS OF AN OYSTER

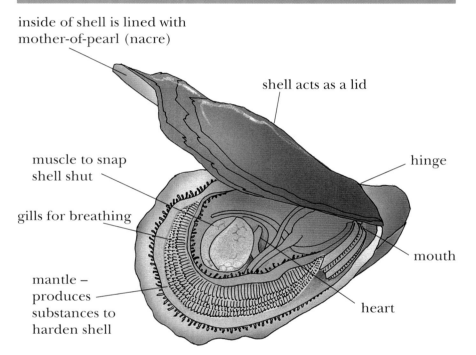

inside of shell is lined with mother-of-pearl (nacre)

shell acts as a lid

muscle to snap shell shut

gills for breathing

mantle – produces substances to harden shell

hinge

mouth

heart

Oysters are found in the mild or warm sea waters of the world.

FOOD

An oyster feeds by filtering tiny plants and animals (plankton) from water.

HOW AN OYSTER LIVES

• A female oyster produces over 500 million eggs a year.
• An oyster is as big as a needle head when it hatches. At one month, it is the size of a pea.
• For the first two weeks of its life, an oyster floats and swims until it finds a rock or hard object to fasten to.
• Oysters live for about six years

PEARL OYSTERS

A pearl oyster is one of many kinds of oysters. Pearl oysters make pearls.

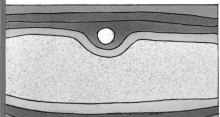 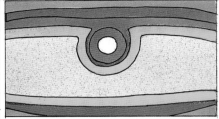 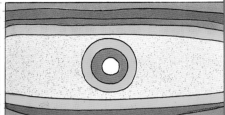

1. Sometimes a piece of sand or grit gets inside the oyster's shell.

2. The oyster produces mother-of-pearl (nacre) to cover the piece of sand.

3. A pearl forms and comes away from the inside of the shell.

OYSTER ENEMIES

An oyster has many enemies.

- The oyster catcher bird can open an oyster's shell with its beak.
- Oyster-drill snails and whelks can bore a hole in the oyster shell and suck out the meat.
- Fish feed on young oysters when they hatch.
- Starfish can pull oyster shells open with their tube feet and eat the oyster inside.

INTERESTING FACT

An oyster's shell is its skeleton. The young of an oyster is called a spat.

OYSTER FARMS ▶

Many people enjoy eating oysters. Most of the oysters people eat come from oyster farms in shallow coastal waters.

PAINTING

SEE ALSO   • Cartoon • Colour

A painting is a picture made using paint and a brush. People paint to express ideas. Painting can give people lots of pleasure. You can use colours, and different kinds of paint and surfaces to make a painting. Every painter has their own way of expressing their feelings and ideas in painting.

KINDS OF PAINT

- Oil paint is sticky and takes a long time to dry. Oil paint can be used on canvas or board.
- Acrylic paint dries quickly. It can be used on paper, canvas and board.
- Watercolour paint is mixed with water. It dries quickly. Watercolour paint is used on paper.
- Gouache paint is like watercolour paint, but you cannot see through it. It can be used like oil paint or mixed with water, like watercolour paint.

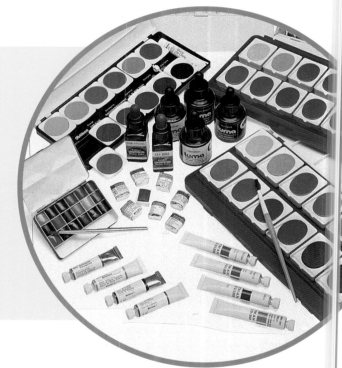

◀ STILL LIFE

A still-life painting is a painting of a single object or a group of objects. Fruit, flowers, dishes or jugs have often been used in still-life paintings by famous artists.

SKETCHING

A sketch is a quick drawing. Painters often use sketches to start a painting. They can paint over the sketch or use it as a guide for their painting.

LANDSCAPES

Some painters paint landscapes. These are outdoor scenes that include trees, sky, clouds, water, hills, towns or cities.

PORTRAITS ▶

A portrait is a painting of a person. Painters often use models when they are painting pictures of people.

◀ ABSTRACT PAINTINGS

An abstract painting is a picture made up of lines, shapes and blocks of colours.

PANDA

| SEE ALSO | • Animal • Bear • Endangered Species • Mammal |

A panda is a mammal. There are two kinds of pandas which are very different. The giant panda looks like a bear. The red panda is much smaller. It is related to the racoon.

PARTS OF A GIANT PANDA

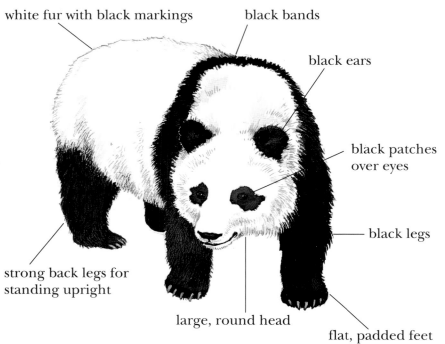

white fur with black markings

black bands

black ears

black patches over eyes

black legs

strong back legs for standing upright

large, round head

flat, padded feet

Length: 100 to 150 centimetres
Weight: 75 to 160 kilograms

HOW GIANT PANDAS LIVE

• Giant pandas usually live alone in bamboo forests. They shelter in caves, hollow trees or rock crevices.
• A female panda gives birth to one or two cubs each year. The cubs are white at birth. By one month old, they have black markings.

FOOD FOR GIANT PANDAS

young, green bamboo shoots

AN ENDANGERED SPECIES

Today, there are only about 700 pandas left on Earth. They only live in the mountain forests of China. Parts of these forests have been made into national parks to save the pandas. In the past, large areas of these forests have been cleared.

PARTS OF A RED PANDA

ears

pale face with reddish brown streaks

reddish brown fur

bushy tail with dark bands

four agile legs

Length: 50 to 60 centimetres
Weight: 3 to 4.5 kilograms

FOOD FOR RED PANDAS

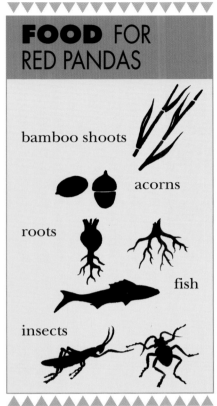

bamboo shoots

acorns

roots

fish

insects

HOW RED PANDAS LIVE

• Red pandas live in pairs or family groups. They sleep in trees during the day, and search for food at dusk and at dawn.

• A female red panda gives birth to one or two cubs each year. The cubs stay with their mother until they are about one year old.

WHERE PANDAS LIVE

● **Giant panda**
China

■ **Red panda**
Eastern Tibet/Nepal

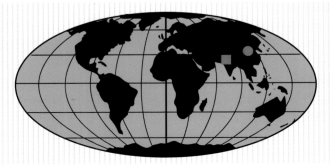

PAPER

SEE ALSO • Book • Newspaper • Printing • Recycling

Paper is made from plant fibres which come from the wood of trees. Books, newspapers, magazines, writing materials and many other things we use are made from paper.

HISTORY

About 5000 years ago, the Egyptians used a plant called papyrus to write on.

The Chinese invented the paper we know about 2000 years ago.

HOW PAPER IS MADE

Today, most paper is made from wood pulp.

1. Trees are cut down and sawn into logs. The logs are sent to the paper mills.

2. At the paper mill, the bark is removed from the logs. The logs are chopped into chips.

RECYCLED PAPER

Using recycled paper saves our forests, uses less energy and helps to reduce air and water pollution.

INTERESTING FACT

Paper can also be made from cotton and rags.

TREES FOR PAPER ▶

Millions of trees are cut down each year to provide enough wood chips to make paper. New trees are planted in their place for the future. It takes many years for a tree to grow before it can be used to make paper.

USES OF PAPER

wallpaper

bank cheques

photographs

books

magazines

newspapers

cardboard packaging

tissues

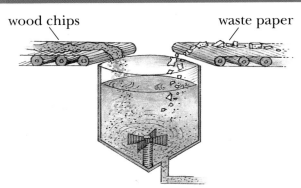

3. The chips are mixed with water and beaten into pulp. Waste paper can be added to the pulping machine to make recycled paper.

wood chips   waste paper

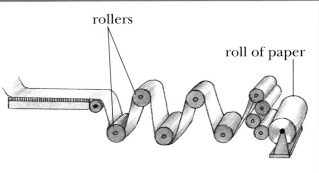

rollers

roll of paper

4. The wet pulp is spread over wire mesh. The pulp passes through a series of rollers that press and dry it. The finished paper is rolled on to a large roll.

PARROTS

SEE ALSO • Animal • Bird

Parrots are a family of birds with brightly-coloured feathers. There are over 320 kinds of parrots. They are many different sizes, shapes and colours.

PARTS OF A GOLDEN-HEADED PARAKEET

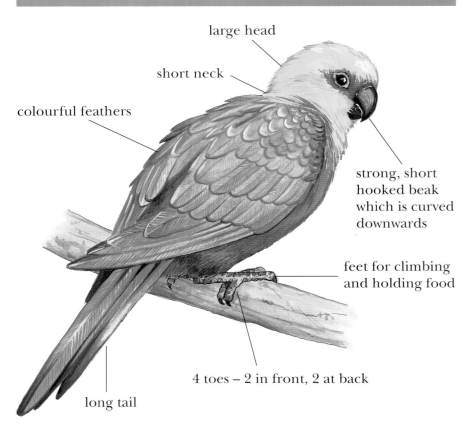

large head

short neck

colourful feathers

strong, short hooked beak which is curved downwards

feet for climbing and holding food

4 toes – 2 in front, 2 at back

long tail

Length: 25 centimetres, including tail

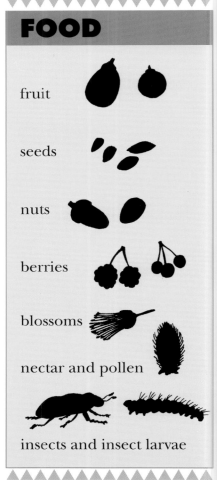

FOOD

fruit

seeds

nuts

berries

blossoms

nectar and pollen

insects and insect larvae

WHERE PARROTS LIVE

● Australia
■ South America
▼ Central America
◆ New Guinea
★ Africa
▲ Indonesia/Malaysia

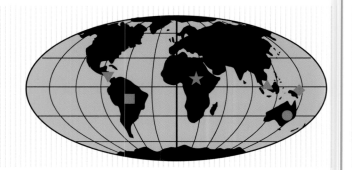

In South-East Asia, hanging parrots sleep upside down in trees.

HOW
PARROTS LIVE
- Parrots usually live in pairs or flocks in forests. They use their beaks to climb through branches and for cracking seeds.
- Parrots build nests in trees, on the ground or in cracks in rocks. Most parrots lay three to four round, white eggs.

KINDS
OF PARROTS

Macaws are the largest parrots. They live in Central and South America. ▶

Budgerigars are parrots. They are a popular cage-bird. In the wild, budgerigars often live in large flocks. ▼

The sulphur-crested cockatoo is an Australian parrot. It has a crest of feathers on its head. ▼

◀ Rainbow lorikeets have smooth, slender beaks. They eat nectar, pollen and fruit.

35

PENGUIN

SEE ALSO • Animal • Antarctica • Bird

A penguin is a bird that cannot fly. Penguins can swim and dive very well. They spend most of their time in water. There are many different kinds of penguins.

PARTS OF AN EMPEROR PENGUIN

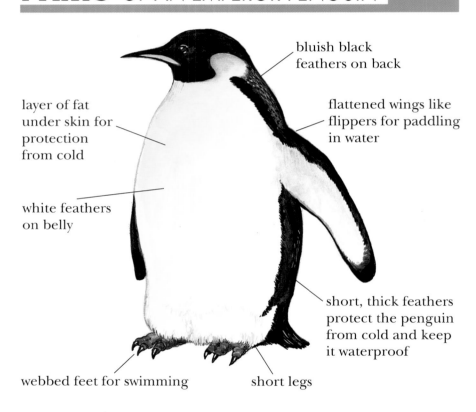

bluish black feathers on back

flattened wings like flippers for paddling in water

layer of fat under skin for protection from cold

white feathers on belly

short, thick feathers protect the penguin from cold and keep it waterproof

webbed feet for swimming

short legs

Penguins vary in size. The emperor penguin is the largest penguin. It is 1.2 metres tall and can weigh up to 50 kilograms.

ROOKERIES
Penguins lay their eggs and raise their young on land. They make their nests in large groups called rookeries.

WHERE PENGUINS LIVE

● Antarctica
■ Australia
◆ New Zealand
★ South Africa
▲ Galápagos Islands

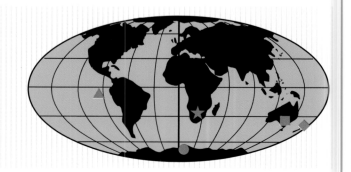

KINDS OF PENGUINS

emperor penguin | fairy penguin | Adélie penguin | chinstrap penguin | Gentoo penguin | macaroni penguin | king penguin

FOOD

fish

HOW PENGUINS ▶ MOVE

Penguins spend most of their time in water. They can leap from the water on to ice. Penguins can move quickly over the ice by sliding on their stomachs.

HOW EMPEROR PENGUINS LIVE

• Emperor penguins live in large groups called colonies.
• The female emperor penguin lays one egg and returns to the sea.
• The male looks after the egg for two months until it hatches. The egg is placed on the top of its feet to protect it from the cold. It is kept in place by a flap of skin.
• The male penguin feeds the chick with food from its crop (throat).
• The adult penguins make a circle around the young chicks to keep them warm.

PET

SEE ALSO
• Canary • Cat • Dog
• Guinea Pig • Rabbit

A pet is an animal that has been tamed.
Almost any animal can be a pet.

HISTORY

• Long ago, the Egyptians trained hyenas as
hunting companions. They also kept cats as
sacred animals.
• During the Middle Ages, people tamed
falcons and other birds of prey, and used them
to hunt.

PETS NEED CARE

Pets need food, shelter
and regular exercise.
If they become sick, they
may need the care of
a veterinarian.

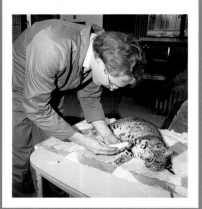

CHOOSING A PET

It is important to choose a pet carefully.
Dogs are the most common pets. A large
dog needs plenty of space to exercise.

KINDS OF PETS

Most animals can become a pet. Some animals need special care. You need to know how they live and behave in the wild.

Terrapins and axolotls are unusual pets.

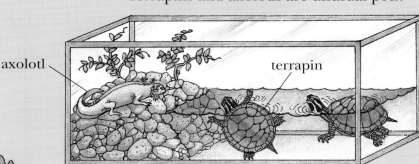

axolotl

terrapin

◄ Lambs, goats, chickens and ducklings are often pets for children who live in the country.

▲

Hamsters, gerbils, guinea pigs and mice are kept in cages and hutches. Caged pets need their cages cleaned regularly.

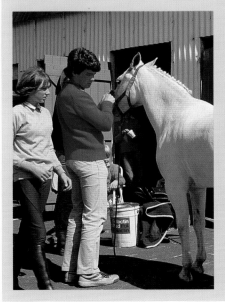

◄ A pony needs lots of space and regular exercise.

▲ Fish are kept as pets in aquariums.

PIGEON

SEE ALSO • Animal • Bird

A pigeon is a bird that belongs in the pigeon and dove family. Pigeons live in parks and cities all over the world.

PARTS OF A COMMON PIGEON

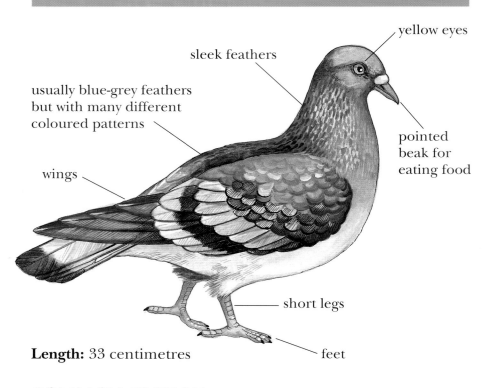

yellow eyes

sleek feathers

usually blue-grey feathers but with many different coloured patterns

wings

pointed beak for eating food

short legs

feet

Length: 33 centimetres

COMMON PIGEON

Other names: rock pigeon, feral pigeon

WHERE PIGEONS LIVE

Pigeons live all over the world except Antarctica.

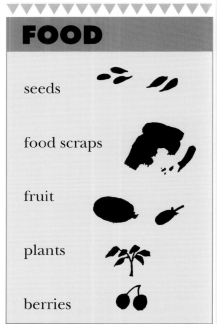

FOOD

seeds

food scraps

fruit

plants

berries

HOW PIGEONS LIVE

• Pigeons make simple nests of twigs and grass.
• Female pigeons lay one or two white eggs.
• Young pigeons are called squabs. Both male and female pigeons help raise the squabs.
• Pigeons live for about 20 years.

KINDS OF PIGEONS

As well as the common pigeon, there are many different kinds of wild pigeons.

The purple-crowned pigeon lives in rain forests. It has purple feathers on its head.
►

The crowned pigeon of New Guinea is one of the largest pigeons. It has lacy tufts of feathers on its head.
▼

The bleeding heart pigeon lives in the Philippines. It has a red patch of feathers on its chest.

Homing pigeons can find their way home over long distances. They are used for racing and to carry messages.
▼

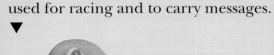

INTERESTING FACT

Unlike other birds, pigeons drink by sucking water. Other birds take a gulp of water and lift their heads to swallow.

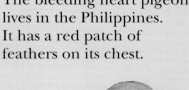

PIRATE

A pirate is a robber who attacks and robs ships at sea. Most pirates roamed the seas long ago. There are still dangerous pirates in some parts of the world today.

SEE ALSO
• Flag

INFAMOUS ▶ PIRATES

Edward Teach was a terrifying pirate. He was known as Captain Blackbeard. In battle, he carried six pistols and had burning matches twisted in his hair. He died on a British warship in 1718.

Anne Bonney and Mary Read were women pirates. They disguised themselves as men and, with other fierce pirates, attacked other ships.

THE JOLLY ROGER

The Jolly Roger was the pirate flag. It had a white skull and crossbones on a black background.

The Pirate Code was a set of laws for behaviour on a pirate ship.

HOW PIRATES ROBBED SHIPS

Pirates sailed close to the ships they wanted to rob. These ships often carried gold and other treasures. The pirates would jump on board and fight the crew.

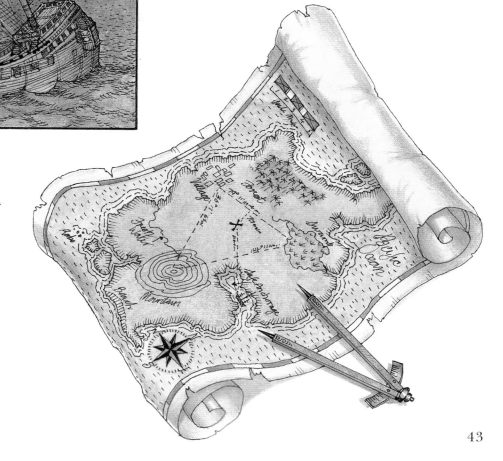

Pirates sailed small, fast ships so they could chase other ships and escape quickly.

PIRATE TREASURE ▶

Pirates hid their loot of gold, silver and jewels in safe places. Maps were made of these secret places so the pirates could find their treasure again. Some people are still searching for hidden pirate treasure.

PLANET

| SEE ALSO | • Astronomy • Earth • Satellite • Star • Sun • Universe |

A planet is a ball of rock, metal and gases which orbits a star. There are nine planets that orbit the Sun which is a star. The Earth is one of them. These nine planets and the Sun make up the solar system.

The planets move in the same direction around the Sun. Each planet has its own path and spins as it moves.

PLANET MOONS

Most planets have small moons orbiting them. The Earth has one moon.

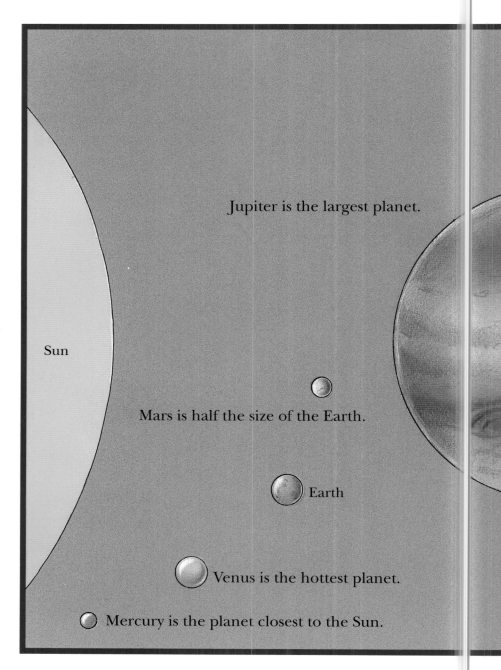

Jupiter is the largest planet.

Sun

Mars is half the size of the Earth.

Earth

Venus is the hottest planet.

Mercury is the planet closest to the Sun.

WATCHING THE PLANETS

People use a telescope to look at stars and planets in the night sky.

- A planet looks like a small, steady disc of light.
- A star looks like a tiny twinkling point of light.

INTERESTING FACT

Planets do not make their own light. They reflect the Sun's light.

ORBIT

An orbit is the path of a planet around the Sun, or the path of a moon around a planet.

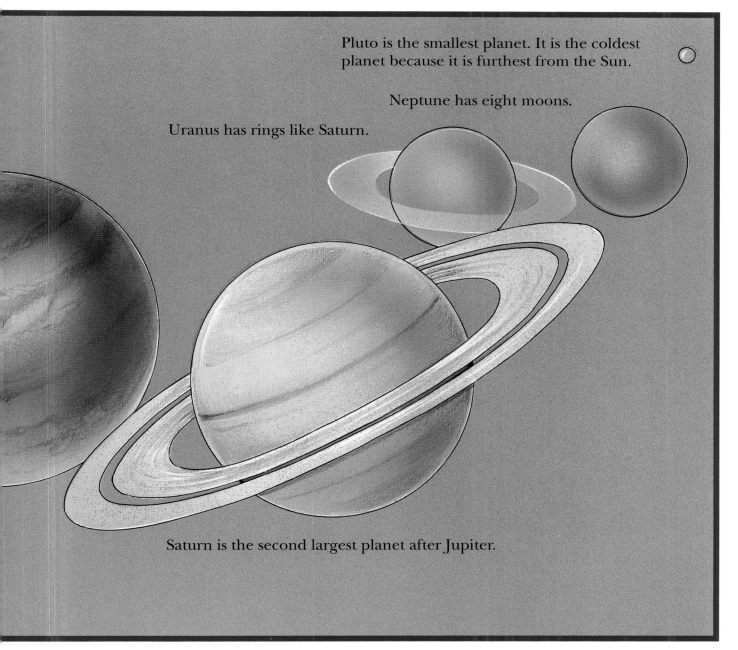

Pluto is the smallest planet. It is the coldest planet because it is furthest from the Sun.

Neptune has eight moons.

Uranus has rings like Saturn.

Saturn is the second largest planet after Jupiter.

PLANT

SEE ALSO • Fern • Flower • Forest • Fruit • Tree

A plant is a living thing that can grow in soil.
Plants make their own food from sunlight and water.
Without plants, there would be no life on Earth.

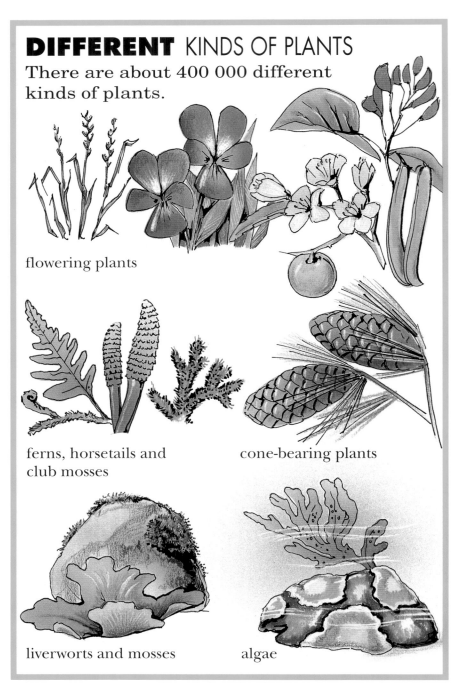

DIFFERENT KINDS OF PLANTS

There are about 400 000 different kinds of plants.

flowering plants

ferns, horsetails and club mosses

cone-bearing plants

liverworts and mosses

algae

PLANTS ARE USEFUL

- The oxygen in the air we breathe comes from plants.
- The food we eat comes from plants or from the animals that eat plants.
- Plants provide us with clothing and shelter.
- Many medicines come from plants.

All plants need air, water and sunlight to make food. They use a process called photosynthesis to make their food.

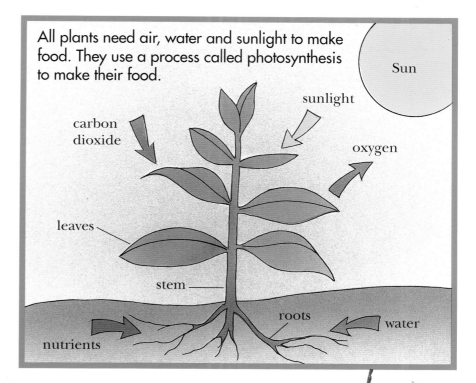

carbon dioxide

sunlight

Sun

oxygen

leaves

stem

roots

water

nutrients

INTERESTING FACT

The largest plant is the giant sequoia tree. It can grow to 112 metres tall. The smallest flowering plant is duckweed. It is only 0.6 millimetres long.

INSECT-EATING ▶ PLANTS

Some plants eat insects. The venus flytrap is an insect-eating plant.

PLASTIC

SEE ALSO | • Coal • Oil • Pollution

Plastic is a material that is made from chemicals.
Plastic can easily be made into any shape.
It does not rust or rot.

SOME PLASTIC PRODUCTS

toys

plates

bowls, cups, saucers

bottles

bags and packaging

telephone

HOW PLASTIC OBJECTS ARE MADE

Plastics are made from chemicals in factories. The
chemicals come from coal, oil, wood and natural gas.
Plastic products are made in moulds, or shaped
by blowing.

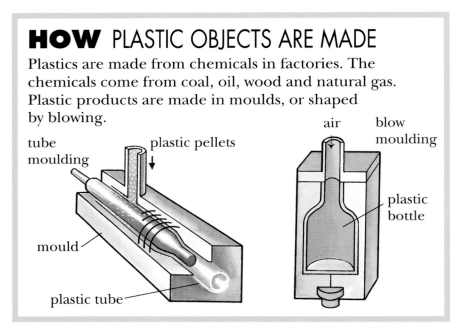

tube
moulding

plastic pellets

mould

plastic tube

air

blow
moulding

plastic
bottle

PLASTIC WASTE

Most plastic products can
be recycled and reused.
Plastic waste does not break
down. It pollutes the
natural environment.

INTERESTING FACT

Bakelite was the first
plastic used to make
many objects. It was
invented by Leo
Baekeland in 1909.

PLATYPUS

SEE ALSO • Animal • Mammal

A platypus is an egg-laying mammal.
It only lives in Australia.

PARTS OF A PLATYPUS

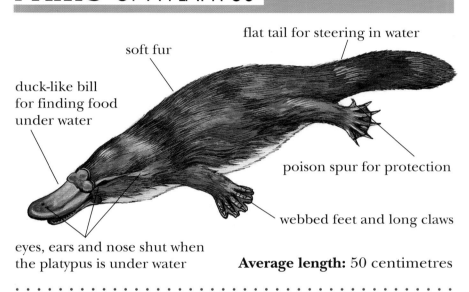

flat tail for steering in water

soft fur

duck-like bill
for finding food
under water

poison spur for protection

webbed feet and long claws

eyes, ears and nose shut when
the platypus is under water

Average length: 50 centimetres

HOW PLATYPUSES LIVE

• Platypuses live in rivers, streams and
freshwater lakes. They nest in burrows in
the river bank.
• The female platypus lays between one and
three soft leathery eggs. The eggs hatch after
ten days. The young feed on milk from their
mother for up to four months.

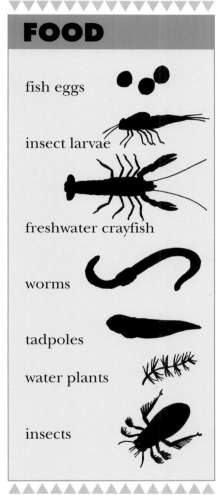

FOOD

fish eggs

insect larvae

freshwater crayfish

worms

tadpoles

water plants

insects

PROTECTING THE PLATYPUS

The platypus is a protected
animal. In the past, many have
been killed for their fur.
We must protect the natural
places where platypuses live
to save them.

POLICE

Police are people who prevent crime, and keep law and order. Laws protect the rights of people in a country. Police have many different duties. Most police wear uniforms so people can recognize them.

SEE ALSO

• Clothes

FINGERPRINTS

Every person's fingerprints are different. Detectives look for fingerprints at the scene of a crime. Brushing special powder on shiny surfaces shows up fingerprints.

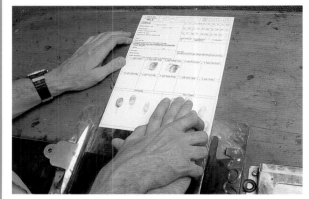

STREET PATROLS

Police patrol the streets either on foot or in vehicles to prevent crime.

EDUCATION ▲ PROGRAMMES

Police visit schools. They help children understand the laws of their country.

POLICE COMMUNICATIONS

Police use computers and satellites to send information about crimes around the world very quickly.

Police often help people to find places.

TRAFFIC POLICE

Uniformed police often direct traffic.

DETECTIVES

Detectives try to solve crimes. They use many scientific aids. They interview eyewitnesses (people who have seen a crime). The descriptions from eyewitnesses are used to build up a picture of the suspect.

Transport police patrol the roads and help keep them safe.

POLICE DOGS ▶

Police dogs are trained to track down and capture criminals. They can help the police search for drugs.

POLLUTION

SEE ALSO • Conservation • Ecolog[y] • Food Chain • Recyclin[g]

Pollution damages the air, water and soil. It is caused by waste and poisons that are released into the water and air, and dumped on land.

AIR POLLUTION ▶

All living things need air to stay alive. Polluted air can make plants, animals and people ill. Smoke from factories contains poisons which pollute the air.

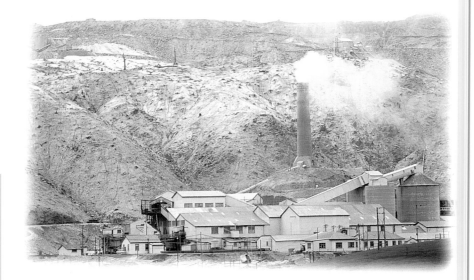

WATER POLLUTION

Rivers, lakes and oceans are home for many living things. Water pollution poisons the water and kills the things that live there.

SOIL POLLUTION

The soil and land can be polluted in different ways. Litter is one kind of land pollution. Chemicals are sprayed on plants to kill insects and weeds. This pollutes the land.

THE FOOD CHAIN

Poisons can be passed along a food chain.

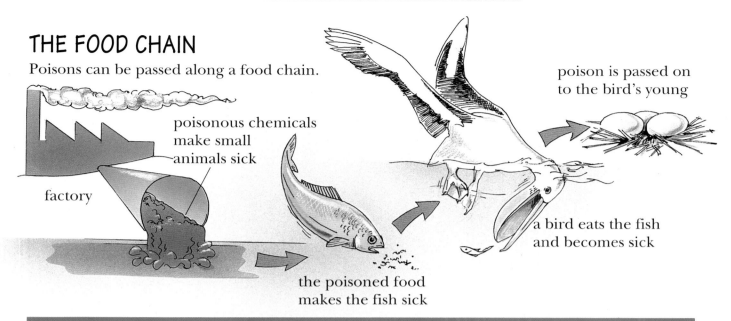

poisonous chemicals make small animals sick

factory

poison is passed on to the bird's young

a bird eats the fish and becomes sick

the poisoned food makes the fish sick

WAYS TO STOP POLLUTION

Many countries have laws to stop pollution.
We can help to reduce pollution by:

- composting food scraps
- re-using things instead of throwing them away
- recycling paper, glass and plastic
- using products that do not poison the environment.

SMOG

Smog is a mixture of smoke and fog.
In large cities, smog hangs like a cloud.

POND LIFE

SEE ALSO
• Ecology • Fish • Frog
• Insect

A pond is a small body of shallow, fresh water. Ponds provide a home for many living things.

SOME KINDS OF POND LIFE

dragonfly

frog

mayfly

frog spawn

tadpoles

water boatman

freshwater crayfish

fish

diving beetle

platypus

worm

Different animals live in different parts of a pond.
• Birds live in the trees around the pond.
• Frogs and platypuses live on and in the mud banks.
• Insects and pond snails live on water plants around and in the pond.
• Crayfish live under rocks at the bottom of the pond.
• Worms live in mud at the bottom of the pond.
• Diving beetles catch prey under water.
• Fish and tadpoles live in the open water.

POND WATER
Pond water can be:
• clear
• muddy
• cloudy
• frothy
• green and slimy.

The animals that live in a pond are affected by many things:

- light
- water temperature
- depth and flow of water
- slope of banks
- pollution
- material on the bottom – stone, mud or sand.

bird

pond snail

stonefly nymph

FOOD IN A POND

- Plants floating on the water's surface or growing at the edge of the pond provide food for plant-eating animals (herbivores).
- Plant-eating animals provide food for meat-eating animals (carnivores).
- Other kinds of food are washed into the pond.

FROGS ▼

Frogs feed on insects around a pond. They lay their eggs in the pond.

INTERESTING FACT

Insects are common in ponds. Some come to the surface to breathe, others have gills.

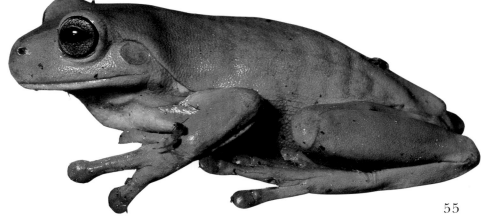

POSTAL SERVICE

SEE ALSO • Hobby • Transport

The postal service carries letters, cards and packages from a sender to a receiver who may be anywhere in the world.

HISTORY

In the past, messages were delivered by people who could run fast from one place to another.

Sir Roland Hill introduced the stick-on stamp in England in 1840. All stamps cost one penny. He thought more people would use the post if it was cheap. Before this, postal services were very expensive.

INTERESTING FACT

Lots of people collect stamps for a hobby. They are called philatelists. Some stamps are valuable because they are rare.

POSTAL SERVICE

POSTING A LETTER

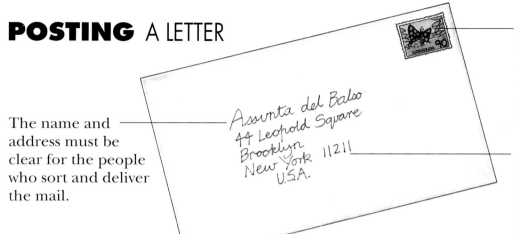

The name and address must be clear for the people who sort and deliver the mail.

Stamps are put in the top right-hand corner. Stamps cost different amounts depending on where a letter is going.

A postcode is a numbered code for an area. Postcodes make it easy to sort and deliver mail.

WHAT HAPPENS TO YOUR LETTER?

Each letter is sorted several times before it finally reaches its destination.

1. Letters are posted at a post box or at the post office.

2. The mail is collected from post boxes and taken to the post office to be sorted.

3. Machines sort the mail into countries and cities.

4. Mail is taken to different areas by air, sea, van, bicycle or on foot.

5. Finally, letters are sorted by street and house number, and the letter is delivered.

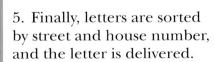

PRINTING

SEE ALSO
• Book • Library
• Newspaper • Paper

Printing is a way of making copies of the same work. Thousands of years ago, printing was done by hand. Today, machines are used to print books, magazines and newspapers.

HISTORY

The first books were printed in China and Japan about 2000 years ago. Words were carved in wooden blocks. The block was inked and pressed on a piece of paper.

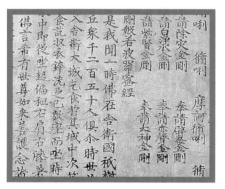

In the 1400s, Johannes Gutenberg set up the first printing press and printed the first book in Europe. He made up a plate for each page using metal blocks. Each block was a single letter. The letters were arranged to make words.

MODERN
PRINTING PRESSES

Johannes Gutenberg's printing methods were the beginning of modern printing.

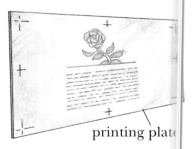

printing plate

• Computers are used to put letters together, and to design and lay out pages.

• The page layouts are used to make the printing plates.

PRINTING IN COLOUR

Printing presses can print in many different colours and on many different materials.

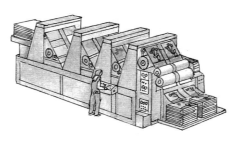
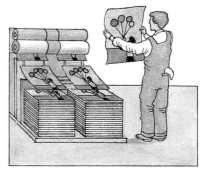

1. A colour picture is made up of four colours: yellow, magenta (red), cyan (blue) and black.

2. As paper runs through a press, the four colours are added on ink rollers, one after another. Black is printed last.

3. The paper comes out at the other end as printed pages in full colour.

Printing is part of our everyday life.

paper

printing plate

• Printing presses apply ink to paper.

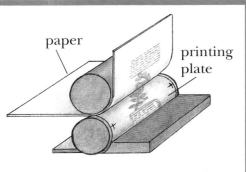

newspaper

timetable

advertisement

book

magazine

pamphlet

brochure

cheque/banknote

map

birthday card

diary

membership card

label

billboard

PUPPET

SEE ALSO • Doll • Drama • Toy

A puppet is a figure which can be moved by a person. A puppet show is one of the oldest kinds of entertainment. There are many different kinds of puppets.

HISTORY

Punch-and-Judy shows have been popular in Europe for hundreds of years. The shows were performed in holiday towns to entertain children.

STRING PUPPETS

String puppets are called marionettes. The strings are attached to a wooden bar. The puppet is controlled by moving the wooden bar.

◀ FINGER PUPPETS

Finger puppets are easy to make. You can make different characters for the fingers of your hand and present a puppet play.

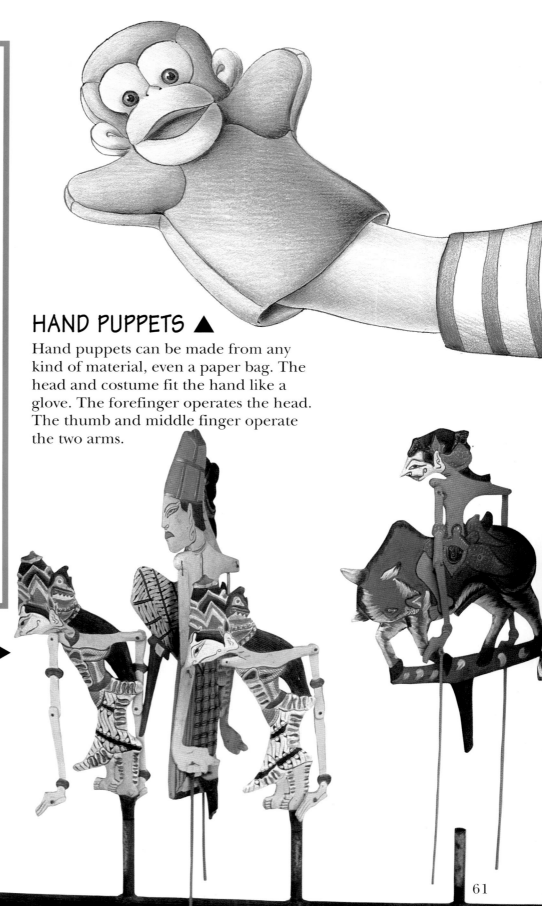

HAND PUPPETS ▲

Hand puppets can be made from any kind of material, even a paper bag. The head and costume fit the hand like a glove. The forefinger operates the head. The thumb and middle finger operate the two arms.

BODY PUPPETS

Life-sized puppets are light and easy to move. They are made from foam rubber over a light frame. The person inside the puppet controls the movement. Sometimes electronic devices are used to control facial movements.

SHADOW PUPPETS ▶

Shadow puppet theatre has been performed in Asia for thousands of years. The puppets are flat. They are held close to a screen. The light behind the puppets casts a shadow which the audience sees from the other side of the screen.

QUAIL

SEE ALSO
• Animal • Bird

A quail is a small, plump bird. Quails live in grassy areas on most continents. They only fly for short distances.

PARTS OF A COMMON QUAIL

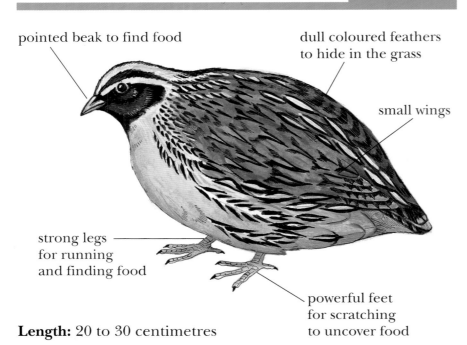

pointed beak to find food

dull coloured feathers to hide in the grass

small wings

strong legs for running and finding food

powerful feet for scratching to uncover food

Length: 20 to 30 centimetres

FOOD

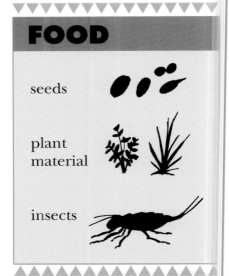

seeds

plant material

insects

QUAIL FARMS
Quails are bred for their eggs and for food.

HOW QUAILS LIVE

• During autumn and winter, quails live in groups called coveys.
• Quails build a grassy nest in the ground.
• The female quail lays 12 to 18 eggs. The male bird keeps the eggs warm until they hatch. The young birds usually stay with their parents for their first summer.
• Quails fly close to the ground. They are hard to see because they hide in the grass.

QUARRY

A quarry is a place where rocks are cut out of the ground. Granite, limestone, marble, slate, gravel, clay and sand are rocks which are quarried.

SEE ALSO
• Gem • Minerals • Mining
• Rock

HISTORY

Long ago, people dug quarries to find flint. They used the flint to make tools and weapons.

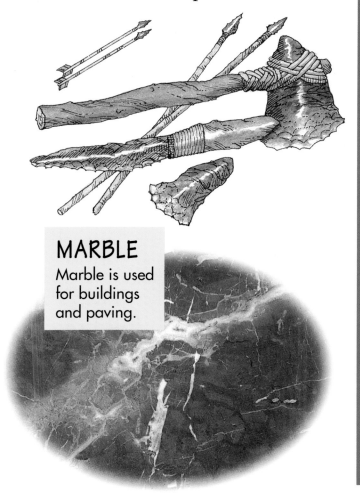

MARBLE
Marble is used for buildings and paving.

HOW ROCK IS QUARRIED

• Hard rocks such as granite are broken into smaller pieces using explosives. Marble, which is a soft rock, is cut using electric cutters, wire saws and drills.

• Bulldozers, diggers, excavators and dredges remove the rocks from the quarry.

• The rocks are taken to crushing plants.

• Crushed rock can be used for railway lines and roads, and cement for concrete buildings.

63

QUARTZ

Quartz is the most common mineral found in the Earth. Pure quartz is clear. It looks like glass. Some kinds of quartz are coloured.

SEE ALSO
• Gem • Minerals • Rock

QUARTZ JEWELS

There are many different kinds of quartz which can be used to make beautiful jewels.

rose coloured quartz

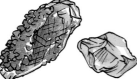
amethyst

citrine

milky quartz

green quartz

A digital clock is regulated by a vibrating quartz crystal. ▶

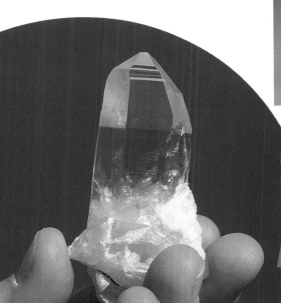

INTERESTING FACT

Quartz crystals look like frozen water. They were named after the Greek word for ice.

USE OF QUARTZ

Quartz is used in many things we need today.

lenses – microscopes

binoculars

glasses

sandpaper

television, radar and radio instruments

electronics

glass products